SKY RANCH FAMILY DEVOTIONALS

OPEN YOUR EYES

Stacy A. Davis, Lisa Clark and Tori Miller

SKY RANCH
TEXAS COLORADO OKLAHOMA

The Sky Ranch Family Devotional Open Your Eyes *is dedicated to all of the Sky Ranch Families*

A Sky Ranch Publication

Sky Ranch
600 North Pearl Street
STE 640, LB 148
Dallas, Texas   75201

All Bible references are from the New American Standard Bible unless otherwise noted.

First Sky Ranch Edition   2011

Manufactured in the United States of America

All content used by permission from Stacy Davis, Lisa Clark and Tori Miller.

ISBN-10   09834-13800
ISBN-13   97809-8341-3806

Foreword

Dear Sky Ranch Families:

Over 55 years ago, God used Mel and Winkie Brewer to spark a fire that became a vision...that was just the beginning. Even the Brewers would agree that Sky Ranch is a 55 year story of a *parade of saints* laying their lives down for kids of His Kingdom that has expanded and grown into leading youth and families to know and follow Christ to where they are leading the next generation. This is what Sky Ranch is all about.

Sky Ranch is a *legacy*, a selfless gift of time, passions, and resources passed down by generations of men and women who were once boys and girls in need of a hero. Although you can try to define it by bricks and sticks or points on the map in three different states, at the end of the day these buildings only mirror the heart and character of the people who have and will live this story.

The work of this devotional is yet another evidence of individuals we'd like to recognize that came together to join the parade of saints to further the legacy of Sky Ranch. We'd like to express a very special thank you to our writers Stacy Davis, Lisa Clark and Tori Miller. We are grateful that they allowed God to work through them to develop this material for our families to utilize as a tool to help strengthen their relationships with the Lord and each other. We appreciate the contributions of Debbie Stuart, Larry Taylor and Chris Witt for their time and help with theologically reviewing the study material and providing their counsel. The need for wisdom and knowledge of publishing was met by the faithful time and talents of Tom Ziglar, Laurie Magers and Bruce Barbour. Finally, we are grateful for a very special family, one that humbly wishes to remain anonymous, one that has consistently shared their blessings with Sky Ranch in so many ways, including the funding of this project.

The impact of camp ministry is proven to be one of the most effective ministries for youth today. It is our desire that no child ever be denied the opportunity to come to camp. The proceeds for this book will be used to fund scholarships for those that would not have the opportunity to encounter Sky Ranch without the help of others to fund the experience.

It is our prayer that through this work, lives will be transformed, individuals and families will be strengthened through the power of God's truth, and lives will be impacted for eternity. You are all a blessing to Sky Ranch and it is a privilege to serve you.

> In His grip,
> Linda S. Paulk
> President and CEO
> Sky Ranch

SKY RANCH MOTTO:

Impacting Lives Forever!

SKY RANCH MISSION:

Leading youth and families to know and follow Christ

SKY RANCH VISION:

Sky Ranch youth and families are leading the next generation

Introduction

Welcome to a Sky Ranch Family Time! This Family Time Devotional was designed so that the camper can take a piece of Sky Ranch home! It was written by three Sky Ranch moms (Sky-Moms)…Stacy Davis, Tori Miller and Lisa Clark, who all have a heart for encouraging family growth with the Lord. Each writer has a history of ministering to families in their communities and wants to encourage your family. At Sky Ranch, we have seen the many statistics that show the time spent sharing as a family directly impacts the well-being of children in a family. We want to encourage parents to take the time to mentor and share their Biblical values with their kids and the result will be mentally, emotionally, spiritually and physically stronger kids and families.

The study is designed to be used over a 12-month period. Each month a topic is covered that focuses on "God…who is He and what does He do?" It is designed for the family to meet once a month, reading through all five family times at once, or weekly. If you prefer weekly, it can be broken down into either four or five weeks, depending on the month. If your family is new to Bible study, we recommend beginning with a short time period at first, 15-20 minutes or less.

The Bible study is based on the curriculum of the Sky Ranch campers so that the camper or the camper's family can continue the Sky Ranch "family time" at home. We have included a leader guide at the end of each month to encourage or aid the discussions. Mom, Dad, or kids can take turns leading the discussion, encouraging and training everyone to teach others. Encourage the younger ones to listen if they can, but they may need an activity to do. As they get older, they will eventually join in.

We hope that "family time" will become a weekly habit in your home. After the discussion, families can use the time to prepare for the week, make group decisions about upcoming events, or have "game night," playing board games or group video games together. The point is to have a consistent time of meeting to look at God's Word, discuss it and apply it to your life while communicating, having fun, and encouraging the family unit. We hope that you enjoy your "family time"!

Table of contents

MONTH 1

Directions:
As a group, either go through all five "family times" at one time or break it up over four-five weeks, depending on the month.

First – Talk with God

God speaks to you…read the passages and answer the questions.

Reading God's Word, the Holy Bible, is God's way of telling us how to live life. Give Him the time to speak to you. Read the passage first all the way through. Then go back and answer the questions.

Then – Walk with God

Walking…is the action of moving forward with God's instruction from your talk with Him.

And Pray – don't skip this part!

Praying…is your time to talk to God. Prayer is the system that God has designed for you to ask for God's help and you are able to ask because of your relationship with God's only begotten Son, Jesus Christ. If you want to walk with God and hear His direction for you, then you have to ask Him to help you.

For more family activities and devotional ideas to help bring your time in the Word to life, please visit the Sky Ranch Family Devo Resource page. There you will find supplemental activities for each section of the devotional.

www.skyranch.org/familydevoresource

OPEN YOUR EYES

Family Time 1:

Month 1 Topic: God is the Creator, not the created, and different than anything we know...God made you and cares

Talk with God: Read...Genesis 1:1, Isaiah 40:28, 1 Peter 5:7

Genesis 1:1 In the beginning, God created heaven and earth.

- In Gen 1:1, what did God create?

Isaiah 40:28 Do you not know? Have you not heard? The Everlasting God, the Lord, the Creator of the ends of the earth, does not become weary or tired. His understanding is inscrutable.

- In Is 40:28, what does God not do?

1 Peter 5:7 Casting all your anxiety upon Him, because He cares for you.

- In 1 Pet 5:7, who does God care for?

Walk with God: Discuss... Google or look online for a video of outer space, planets, solar system. Look at how big all of it is and notice how small you are in comparison. How does it make you feel that God created so many large things and created you who are so small, and He cares very deeply for you? And since He doesn't weary or tire, how would that affect His care for you? What has happened in your life that tells you that God cares for you?

Prayer suggestion... Pray for God to help you understand how much He cares for you.

Family Time 2:

Month 1 Topic: God is the Creator, not the created, and different than anything we know…Understanding God

Talk with God: Read…Romans 1:20

> **Romans 1:20 For since the creation of the world His invisible attributes, His eternal power and divine nature, have been clearly seen, being understood through what has been made, so that they are without excuse.**

- In Rom 1:20, how long have we been able to clearly see God's divine nature and power?

- In Rom 1:20, how are we to understand God?

Walk with God: Discuss… Go into your back yard or a park…observe God's creation…watch the movement as a flock of birds swoops in unison, or ants as they work as a unit to bring food home…notice the order and structure of God's design. We are to understand God through what He has made. How does this help you understand God better?

Prayer suggestion… Pray for God to help you see proof of Him in creation and give you a better understanding of Him.

Family Time 3:

Month 1 Topic: God is the Creator, not the created, and different than anything we know…Evidence of God

Talk with God: Read…Colossians 1:15, John 4:24, Hebrews 11:1

Colossians 1:15 And He is the image of the invisible God.

- In Col 1:15, what does God look like?

John 4:24 God is a Spirit: and they that worship Him must worship Him in spirit and in truth.

- In John 4:24, what is God?

Hebrews 11:1 Now faith is the assurance of [things] hoped for, the conviction of things not seen.

- In Heb 11:1, what is faith the conviction of?

Walk with God: Discuss… Since God is invisible, it can be hard to trust what you can't see. Share with each other the first time you saw the evidence of God in something…what was it?

Prayer suggestion… Pray for God to strengthen your faith in Him.

Family Time 4:

Month 1 Topic: God is the Creator, not the created, and different than anything we know…All things held together by God

Talk with God: Read…Colossians 1:17, Isaiah 42:5

Colossians 1:17 And He is before all things, and in Him all things hold together.

- In Col 1:17, how is everything held together?

Isaiah 42:5 Thus says God the Lord, Who created the heavens and stretched them out, Who spread out the earth and its offspring, Who gives breath to the people on it, and spirit to those who walk in it.

- In Is 42:5, who gives breath and spirit to the people?

Walk with God: Discuss… Try to think of some amazing things that are held together by God, for example, the sun floating in the sky. What else can you think of?

Prayer suggestion… Pray for God to hold your life together.

Family Time 5:

Month 1 Topic: God is the Creator, not the created, and different than anything we know…God's other creations

Talk with God: Read…Jeremiah 10:12, Romans 11:33-36

> **Jeremiah 10:12** [It is] He who made the earth by His power, Who established the world by His wisdom; and by His understanding He has stretched out the heavens.

- In Jer 10:12, what did God use to make the world?

- What did God use to establish the world and stretch the heavens?

> **Romans 11:33-36** Oh, the depth of the riches both of the wisdom and knowledge of God! How unsearchable are His judgments and unfathomable His ways! (34) For who has known the mind of the Lord, or who became His counselor?

- In Rom 11:34, can anyone know God's mind?

Walk with God: Discuss… Have you noticed that God is really smart? Each person in your family is specifically created by God; it was His choice to make them. What are some good things that you have noticed about the person to your right?

Prayer suggestion… Pray and ask God to guide you with His great wisdom.

Leader Answers:

Month 1 Topic: God is the Creator, not the created, and different than anything we know

Family Time 1:

Leader Answers:

- Heaven and earth
- Weary or tire
- You
- Discussion ideas: The idea of God caring for and loving specifically you can be difficult to accept. And the idea that He never stops caring and doesn't have something more important to think about can be hard to believe, too. But these are promises from Him. Also, Isaiah 49:14-16 says God will not forget you, Isaiah 42:6 says God will hold you by the hand and watch over you. When God gives His word, believe it.

Family Time 2:

Leader Answers:

- Since the creation of the world
- Through what has been made
- Discussion ideas: God's name in the Old Testament is "I am" (Exodus 3:14)… do you know what that translates to? "I exist." God does exist and the evidence of Him is His creation. God is a God of order. Think about your DNA…your genetic code…that is written and is specific to you. God did that!

Family Time 3:

Leader Answers:

- Invisible
- A Spirit
- Things not seen

- Discussion ideas: Give examples, i.e., you asked for a prayer request to be answered and He answered. You prayed for God to show you something in Scripture and you turned right to it. You needed a hug and God prompted someone to hug you. You had a need and God sent someone to bring you dinner, encouragement, direction, etc. There can be many ways we see evidence of Him. There is no coincidence with God; it is all planned. Sometimes we just need to look a little harder and we will see Him.

Family Time 4:

Leader Answers:
- In Him
- God
- Discussion ideas: Another idea that is amazing is YOU! Discuss how detailed people are. What about the detail of our lives we live? Notice how God brings people into our lives to challenge us, direct us, teach us. There is always a plan and He holds it all together.

Family Time 5:

Leader Answers:
- Power
- Wisdom, understanding
- No
- Discussion ideas: Build each other up, or feelings can get hurt. Truly compliment each other by telling of the kindness, encouragement, helpfulness, dedication seen…and don't skip Mom and Dad. Psalm 139:14 tells us we are wonderfully made by God!

MONTH 2

Directions:
As a group, either go through all five "family times" at one time or break it up over four-five weeks, depending on the month.

First – Talk with God

God speaks to you…read the passages and answer the questions.

Reading God's Word, the Holy Bible, is God's way of telling us how to live life. Give Him the time to speak to you. Read the passage first all the way through. Then go back and answer the questions.

Then – Walk with God

Walking…is the action of moving forward with God's instruction from your talk with Him.

And Pray – don't skip this part!

Praying…is your time to talk to God. Prayer is the system that God has designed for you to ask for God's help and you are able to ask because of your relationship with God's only begotten Son, Jesus Christ. If you want to walk with God and hear His direction for you, then you have to ask Him to help you.

For more family activities and devotional ideas to help bring your time in the Word to life, please visit the Sky Ranch Family Devo Resource page. There you will find supplemental activities for each section of the devotional.

www.skyranch.org/familydevoresource

Family Time 1:

Month 2 Topic: God is forever and does not change…Questions/understanding God

Talk with God: Read…Psalm 90:2, Hebrews 1:12

> **Psalm 90:2** Before the mountains were born, or You gave birth to the earth and the world, even from everlasting to everlasting, You are God.

- In Ps 90:2, God was here before what was born?

> **Hebrews 1:12** And like a mantle You will roll them up; like a garment they will also be changed. But You are the same, and Your years will not come to an end.

- In Heb 1:12, will God's years come to an end?

Walk with God: Discuss… "God, where did You come from?" Don't you think this is one of the main questions that everyone has? Scripture tells us that He has always existed and will always exist. This is a tough concept for a group where everything begins and ends. Have you wondered this before? What other questions do you have for God?

Prayer suggestion… Pray that God will help you understand Him better.

Family Time 2:

Month 2 Topic: God is forever and does not change…Gifts from God

Talk with God: Read…James 1:17, Malachi 3:6, Romans 6:23

James 1:17 **Every good thing given and every perfect gift is from above, coming down from the Father of lights, with Whom there is no variation or shifting shadow.**

- In James 1:17, does God vary from Who He is?

- In James 1:17, what comes from God?

Malachi 3:6 **For I, the Lord, do not change; therefore you, O sons of Jacob, are not consumed.**

- In Mal 3:6, what does God promise that He does not do?

Romans 6:23 **For the wages of sin is death, but the free gift of God is eternal life in Christ Jesus our Lord.**

- In Rom 6:23, what is the free gift of God?

Walk with God: Discuss… God is showing us that He gives good, perfect gifts to us and He will not change who He is. Most people might think of gifts from God as home, family, friends -- and they are. But God gives us spiritual gifts as well, like eternal life. How do you receive God's free gift of eternal life?

Prayer suggestion… Pray to receive God's free gift of eternal life.

Family Time 3:

Month 2 Topic: God is forever and does not change…God's views

Talk with God: Read…1 Samuel 15:29, Psalm 45:6, Revelation 4:10

> **1 Samuel 15:29 And also the Glory of Israel will not lie or change His mind; for He is not a man that He should change His mind.**

- In 1 Sam15:29, will God lie?

> **Psalm 45:6 Your throne, O God, is forever and ever; a scepter of uprightness is the scepter of Your kingdom.**

- In Ps 45:6, what is His scepter of?

> **Revelation 4:10 The twenty-four elders will fall down before Him who sits on the throne, and will worship Him Who lives forever and ever.**

- In Rev 4:10, what are the 24 elders falling down before?

Walk with God: Discuss… Scripture explains that God is a King and on a throne with a rod or scepter. He rules by uprightness or "what is right." We also see a promise that God will not lie. Do people and God always match in their views of "what is right"? What if people oppose God? If God does not lie, then who is lying when views oppose each other? Can you think of ideas taught by our society today that oppose God's Word?

Prayer suggestion… Pray for God to help you learn what is right.

Family Time 4:

Month 2 Topic: God is forever and does not change...Calling out/ God's answer

Talk with God: Read...Psalm 4:1, Genesis 21:33, Zechariah 13:9

Psalm 4:1 (David is speaking) Answer me when I call, O God of my righteousness! Thou hast relieved me in my distress; be gracious to me and hear my prayer.

- In Ps 4:1, what is David's other name for a prayer?

Genesis 21:33 And [Abraham] planted a tamarisk tree at Beersheba, and there he called on the name of the Lord, the Everlasting God.

- In Gen 21:33, how did Abraham reach out to God?

Zechariah 13:9 They will call on My name, and I will answer them; I will say, "They are My people," and they will say, "The Lord is my God."

- In Zech 13:9, does God say He will answer His people?

Walk with God: Discuss... The everlasting God promises that He hears and answers. Abraham called out to God. Isn't calling out and praying the same? Do you pray? God will answer His people. But make sure you are calling the right number! Pray to the God Whose Son is Jesus Christ. Pray to the Lord God of Heaven and call on the right name of the Everlasting God. Be patient, God does not always answer us the way we want or in the timing we want. What evidence have you seen of prayer working and God having heard you?

Prayer suggestion... Pray for God to help you pray.

Family Time 5:

Month 2 Topic: God is forever and does not change…God loves us forever

Talk with God: Read…Romans 16:26, Psalm 103:17

> **Romans 16:26** **The mystery which was hidden…but now is manifested, and by the Scriptures of the prophets, according to the commandment of the eternal God, has been made known to all the nations, [leading] to obedience of faith.**

- In Rom 16:26, what is God described as?

- In Rom 16:26, how are hidden mysteries now manifested (told)?

> **Psalm 103:17** **But the loving-kindness of the Lord is from everlasting to everlasting on those who fear Him and His righteousness to children's children.**

- In Ps 103:17, what of the Lord is from everlasting to everlasting?

Walk with God: Discuss… An eternal God loves us forever. Scriptures help us understand God's love…it is kindness. God desires our highest good and He shows us kindness. God values you and shows you kindness. Imitate Him and show kindness to someone else. What acts of kindness can you commit to do this week?

Prayer suggestion… Pray for God to help you understand how much He loves you.

Leader Answers:

Month 2 Topic: God is forever and does not change

Family Time 1:

Leader Answers:

- Before the mountains, earth or world were formed
- No
- Discussion ideas: No question is too small. Share questions like where did God come from? And why are there mosquitoes? Why different races? Is there life on other planets? Explain that God is not like we are. There are many things that we cannot explain and we just have to accept God at His Word.

Family Time 2:

Leader Answers:

- No
- Every good and perfect gift
- He won't change
- Eternal life in Christ Jesus our Lord
- Discussion ideas: God's gifts can be like ours, but His are better. God offers us life forever in His home, Heaven. But we have to receive His free gift to live in His home in the way that He set up by believing Jesus at His Word. Jesus said that He is God's Son, and He died on the cross in our place to pay the price for us. He came back to life three days later and many people saw Him. Then He went up to His home, Heaven, and if we believe Him, when we leave this earth we can live with Him in Heaven forever. And He will help us as we live our life on earth, too.

Family Time 3:

Leader Answers:

- No
- Uprightness
- God on His throne
- Discussion ideas: We will hear things that contradict God's Word. God tells us that ahead of time so don't be surprised by it. The test is, who will you believe? God tells us who is lying; people are. Make sure you know what God says. What subjects do you want to know about? How much time do you spend in His Word finding out?

Family Time 4:

Leader Answers:

- A call
- Called on the name of the Lord
- Yes
- Discussion ideas: God tells us in Scripture, "You do not have because you do not ask," or "You ask with wrong motives" (James 4:2-3). Prayer is something that you get better at as you do it. Make a list to pray from if that helps you keep your focus. Notice other prayers in Scripture, for example, Matthew 6:9-13, which shows Jesus praying to His Father, asking for daily needs, protection from evil, God's will, etc.

Family Time 5:

Leader Answers:

- Eternal
- In the Scriptures or the Commandments of God
- His loving-kindness
- Discussion ideas: Suggestions -- share something important to you, surprise someone by doing their chore for them and letting them get recognition for it, writing a nice note to someone and leaving it at the breakfast table for them in the morning, giving someone a hug, complimenting them, etc.

MONTH 3

Directions:

As a group, either go through all five "family times" at one time or break it up over four-five weeks, depending on the month.

First – Talk with God

> God speaks to you…read the passages and answer the questions.

> Reading God's Word, the Holy Bible, is God's way of telling us how to live life. Give Him the time to speak to you. Read the passage first all the way through. Then go back and answer the questions.

Then – Walk with God

> Walking…is the action of moving forward with God's instruction from your talk with Him.

And Pray – don't skip this part!

> Praying…is your time to talk to God. Prayer is the system that God has designed for you to ask for God's help and you are able to ask because of your relationship with God's only begotten Son, Jesus Christ. If you want to walk with God and hear His direction for you, then you have to ask Him to help you.

For more family activities and devotional ideas to help bring your time in the Word to life, please visit the Sky Ranch Family Devo Resource page. There you will find supplemental activities for each section of the devotional.

www.skyranch.org/familydevoresource

Family Time 1:

Month 3 Topic: God can do anything because God made everything…Noticing/meeting needs

Talk with God: Read…Jeremiah 32:17, Romans 4:17

Jeremiah 32:17   Ah Lord GOD! Behold, You have made the heaven and the earth by Your great power and by Your stretched out arm, and there is nothing too difficult for You.

- In Jer 32:17, is anything too hard for God?

Romans 4:17 [Even] God, Who gives life to the dead and calls into being that which does not exist.

- In Rom 4:17, what does God call into being?

Walk with God: Discuss… Don't you think this is an amazing statement… "calls into being that which does not exist"? God not only creates, but He invents. God sees what the need is and He meets it and we see nothing is too hard for Him. God sees needs and solutions. We are to imitate Him in our lives. What needs are in your family? What are solutions to those needs?

Prayer suggestion… Pray for God's help to see the needs in your family and ways to solve them.

Family Time 2:

Month 3 Topic: God can do anything because God made everything…God's calendar/your calendar

Talk with God: Read…Matthew 19:26, Genesis 1:14

> **Matthew 19:26 And looking upon [them] Jesus said to them, "With men this is impossible, but with God all things are possible."**

- In Matt 19:26, what things are possible with God?

> **Genesis 1:14 Then God said, "Let there be lights in the expanse of the heavens to separate the day from the night, and let them be for signs, and for seasons, and for days and years."**

- In Gen 1:14, why did God make the lights in the heavens?

Walk with God: Discuss… Did you catch that? God made the lights in the heavens as signs to track the seasons, days and years. It is a form of a calendar. But it is a God-sized calendar which only He could do. God likes order and planning. He has created an orderly world. We should imitate Him in our lives. Do you as a family have a group calendar? As kids age, it can be very helpful. What value is there in planning ahead?

Prayer suggestion… Pray for God's direction and wisdom to make changes to your family schedule.

Family Time 3:

Month 3 Topic: God can do anything because God made everything...Your spirit

Talk with God: Read...Zechariah 12:1

Zechariah 12:1 **[Thus] declares the Lord Who stretches out the heavens, lays the foundation of the earth, and forms the spirit of man within him.**

- In Zech 12:1, what does God form within a man?

Walk with God: Discuss... God forms the spirit of a man. God knows what our spirit needs to be strengthened, developed or refreshed. What is your family's spiritual life like? How much time is spent with God, learning about Him or allowing Him to develop you? Evaluate what you could do as a group to improve spending time in the Bible or praying or having godly discussions. How can you encourage each other to believe God more?

Prayer suggestion... Pray for God to help you believe Him.

Family Time 4:

Month 3 Topic: God can do anything because God made everything...His future/your future

Talk with God: Read...Isaiah 44:24-28

Isaiah 44:24-28

(24) Thus says the Lord, your Redeemer, and the One Who formed you from the womb, "I, the Lord, am the maker of all things, stretching out the heavens by Myself, and spreading out the earth all alone..."

- In v24, what is God the maker of?

- In v24, did anyone help Him?

(26) "Confirming the word of His servant, and performing the purpose of His messengers. [It is I] who says of Jerusalem, 'She shall be inhabited!' and of the cities of Judah, 'They shall be built.' And I will raise up her ruins [again].

(27) "[It is I] who says to the depth of the sea, 'Be dried up!' And I will make your rivers dry.

(28) "[It is I] who says of Cyrus, '[He is] My shepherd! And he will perform all My desire.' And he declares of Jerusalem, 'She will be built,' and of the temple, 'Your foundation will be laid.'"

Walk with God: Discuss... In v26, God is telling us that He decides and causes cities to be built again, and in v28 it is the rulers who will perform His desire. Cyrus was named by Isaiah as a ruler almost 150 years before he lived. God knows the future. He has planned it and thinks about it. We are to imitate Him in our lifestyle. Do you think about your future, your family's future? Have you considered a general plan for the next five years?

Prayer suggestion... Pray for God's direction for your future.

Family Time 5:

Month 3 Topic: God can do anything because God made everything...His boundaries/your boundaries

Talk with God: Read...Psalm 104:5-11

Psalm 104:5-11

(5) He established the earth upon its foundations, so that it will not totter forever and ever.

- In v5, what did God establish so that the earth would not totter?

(6) You covered it with the deep as with a garment; the waters were standing above the mountains.

- In v6, where were the waters standing?

(7) At Your rebuke they fled; at the sound of Your thunder they hurried away.

(8) The mountains rose; the valleys sank down to the place which You established for them.

(9) You set a boundary that they may not pass over; so that they will not return to cover the earth.

- In v9, what did God set to stop the waters?

Walk with God: Discuss... God stabilized the foundation of the earth so that it would not totter and created the boundaries of the ocean so that it would not flood the land. God holds it all in place and it keeps the peace. God has good ideas...we need to imitate Him. Does your family have boundaries? Do you have rules that keep the peace? Do you expect respect for each other or your things? Discuss any boundaries that need to be established in your home.

Prayer suggestion... Pray for God to provide the needed family boundaries.

Leader Answers:

Month 3 Topic: God can do anything because God made everything

Family Time 1:
Leader Answers:
- No
- Things which do not exist
- Discussion ideas: Family needs can be a system for organizing...laundry, schedules, family time, homework...or it can be time for talks preparing kids for choosing friends, dating or college. Half of the solution is recognizing the problem. The other half of the solution is creating a way to solve the problem and doing it. Mother/Daughter or Father/Son retreats are ideal for special talks.

Family Time 2:
Leader Answers:
- All
- To separate the day from the night and for signs, seasons, days, years
- Discussion ideas: Families need a main calendar that tracks events for the group. A paper calendar works well in a central place so everyone can see it. A weekly family time is a great place to discuss events and communicate with the group. It can keep life more peaceful, especially if you notice things getting too busy. Then try cancelling events; if not active enough, try scheduling more to do. Find the balance of activity that is right for your family.

Family Time 3:

Leader Answers:

- His spirit
- Discussion ideas: Individual study really helps the group discussion. There are ways to study the Bible for yourself, or a family member may want to go further in self-taught Bible study. Encourage each other to join a Bible study. Being in a community of Christians also teaches us a lot, and that can add to the family time discussion. Look at your church website for class ideas.

Family Time 4:

Leader Answers:

- All things
- No
- Discussion ideas: Will everyone still be in school in five years? Are there any educational trips or fun trips that the family would like to take? Do you need to start saving money now to take them? A five-year plan can help you set goals and a way to accomplish the goals.

Family Time 5:

Leader Answers:

- Foundations
- Above the mountains
- A boundary
- Discussion ideas: In families boundaries matter...can one sibling take an item without asking? What is the result if they do? Usually it is not good. What about privacy? Do people knock before opening a door? What about respect? How does everyone talk to each other? How are kids allowed to talk to parents? How do parents talk to kids? Sometimes we say too much, thinking we are helping, but really we are hurting the other person...just consider how you would want to be treated.

MONTH 4

Directions:

As a group, either go through all five "family times" at one time or break it up over four-five weeks, depending on the month.

First – Talk with God

God speaks to you...read the passages and answer the questions.

Reading God's Word, the Holy Bible, is God's way of telling us how to live life. Give Him the time to speak to you. Read the passage first all the way through. Then go back and answer the questions.

Then – Walk with God

Walking...is the action of moving forward with God's instruction from your talk with Him.

And Pray – don't skip this part!

Praying...is your time to talk to God. Prayer is the system that God has designed for you to ask for God's help and you are able to ask because of your relationship with God's only begotten Son, Jesus Christ. If you want to walk with God and hear His direction for you, then you have to ask Him to help you.

For more family activities and devotional ideas to help bring your time in the Word to life, please visit the Sky Ranch Family Devo Resource page. There you will find supplemental activities for each section of the devotional.

www.skyranch.org/familydevoresource

Family Time 1:

Month 4 Topic: God is perfectly good…All that He makes is good

Talk with God: Read…Genesis 1:31, Deuteronomy 32:4

Genesis 1:31 And God saw all that He had made, and behold, it was very good. And there was evening and there was morning, the sixth day.

- In Gen 1:31, how did God view all that He made?

Deuteronomy 32:4 He is the Rock, His work is perfect: for all His ways are judgment: a God of truth and without iniquity, just and right is He.

- In Deut 32:4, how is God's work described?

Walk with God: Discuss… Before sin, God describes His work… you and me…as good. How do you view people? We all sin…we all fall short of the mark that God set for us and it is important to deal with our sins according to Scripture. But our attitude toward people is important, too. How do you view members of your family or friends? Do you see the good or the bad in them?

Prayer suggestion… Pray for God to help you see the good in life.

Family Time 2:

Month 4 Topic: God is perfectly good...God is the Good Shepherd

Talk with God: Read...Luke 18:19, John 10:14

> **Luke 18:19 And Jesus said to him, "Why do you call Me good? No one is good except God alone."**

- In Luke 18:19, who is good?

> **John 10:14 I am the Good Shepherd; and I know My own, and My own know Me, (15) even as the Father knows Me and I know the Father; and I lay down My life for the sheep.**

- In John 10:14, what is Jesus called?
- Who knows Him?

Walk with God: Discuss... In Luke 18:19, why do you think Jesus is questioning the man for calling Him good? Is Jesus saying that He is not good? No, Jesus is showing that He is God in this statement. The man saw that Jesus is good as God is good. In John 10:14, Jesus' own know Him. They listen to His voice. Who do you listen to? Today many voices distract us...TV, radio, movies, books, magazines, friends, even family...all can say the opposite of God. How much time do you spend listening to Jesus' voice? How well do you know Him? Can you tell when it is Jesus speaking?

Prayer suggestion... Pray for God to help you follow Jesus, your Good Shepherd, and know Him.

Family Time 3:

Month 4 Topic: God is perfectly good…Do good like God

Talk with God: Read…Proverbs 3:27, Proverbs 12:2, 3 John 1:11

Proverbs 3:27 Do not withhold good from those to whom it is due, when it is in your power to do [it].

- In Prov 3:27, what are you not to withhold?

Proverbs 12:2 A good man will obtain favor from the Lord.

- In Prov 12:2, what does a good man obtain?

3 John 1:11 Beloved, do not imitate what is evil, but what is good. The one who does good is of God; the one who does evil has not seen God.

- In 3 John 1:11, what are you to imitate?

Walk with God: Discuss… God tells us to "do good" when it is in our power. Think about that. Do you make nice comments, share, invite someone to dinner, give a big tip, smile, encourage? Do you? Most of us skip the small things, don't we? Does God skip it? No, He doesn't miss a moment to be kind and we are to imitate Him. Still give the big things, too…like food or clothes to a shelter, find someone a job, help the homebound with their needs, visit and care for the widows, orphans, sick and needy. Share the gospel. What will you obtain? Favor. Why would you want favor from the Lord?

Prayer suggestion… Pray for God through His Spirit to help you do what is good.

Family Time 4:

Month 4 Topic: God is perfectly good…God's good news

Talk with God: Read…Luke 2:10, Acts 8:12, 1 Corinthians 15:1, 3-8

Luke 2:10 And the angel said to them, "Do not be afraid; for behold, I bring you good news of a great joy which shall be for all the people; (11) for today in the city of David there has been born for you a Savior, who is Christ the Lord."

- In Luke 2:10, what is the angel bringing to them?

Acts 8:12 But when they believed Philip preaching the good news about the Kingdom of God and the name of Jesus Christ, they were being baptized, men and women alike.

- In Acts 8:12, what is Philip preaching?

1 Corinthians 15:1, 3-8 (1) Now I make known to you, brethren, the gospel which I preached to you… (3) For I delivered to you as of first importance what I also received, that Christ died for our sins according to the Scriptures, (4) and that He was buried, and that He was raised on the third day according to the Scriptures, (5) and that He appeared to Cephas, then to the twelve. (6) After that He appeared to more than five hundred brethren at one time, most of whom remain until now, but some have fallen asleep; (7) then He appeared to James, then to all the apostles; (8) and last of all, as it were to one untimely born, He appeared to me also.

- In 1 Cor 15:1, 3-8, what is being preached?

Walk with God: Discuss… Do you know what the gospel is? Can you share it? It is God's good news of hope to us. 1 Corinthians 15:1, 3-8, is a great summary of the gospel. As a family, practice saying it to each other and share the difference this good news of the gospel has made in your lives. Make a point to share it also with someone outside your family today.

Prayer suggestion… Pray that God will help you understand and share His good news.

Family Time 5:

Month 4 Topic: God is perfectly good...Be good like God

Talk with God: Read...Matthew 5:48, Hebrews 5:9, Ezekiel 36:27

Matthew 5:48 Therefore you are to be perfect, as your Heavenly Father is perfect.

- In Matt 5:48, what are we to be?

Hebrews 5:9 (of Jesus) And having been made perfect, He became to all those who obey Him the source of eternal salvation.

- In Heb 5:9, what was Jesus made?

Ezekiel 36:27 And I will put My Spirit within you and cause you to walk in My statutes, and you will be careful to observe My ordinances.

- In Ezek 36:27, what does God's Spirit within you cause you to do?

Walk with God: Discuss... Sounds like some pressure, doesn't it? God wants us to strive for perfection and desire to be what God wants us to be. God knows we can't do this on our own. So, He tells us that He puts His Spirit within us to help us. His Spirit will cause us to do what God asks us to do, if we listen to Him. Were you aware that God gives us His Spirit to help us? Can you think of times that you have seen this happen?

Prayer suggestion... Pray that God's Spirit will cause you to seek God's perfection.

Leader Answers:

Month 4 Topic: God is perfectly good

Family Time 1:

Leader Answers:

- Very good
- Perfect
- Discussion ideas: Now we live in a fallen world and Romans 3:12 tells us "none are good...not even one." But we are to seek to be good like God is good. However, we can't be good on our own...we need God's redemption and Holy Spirit to help us live life. In our attitude, it can actually be easier to see the negative, can't it? If someone struggles with always seeing the negative, ask them to find the positive or good in the situation...it can be as simple as training yourself to look for the good.

Family Time 2:

Leader Answers:

- God alone
- The Good Shepherd
- His own
- Discussion ideas: In Scripture God talks a lot about "voices." It is of major concern to Him. Spend time in God's Word (try Proverbs) to help you discern between God's voice and those against God. Pray also, asking for God to help you discern between good and evil, and to help you follow the good.

Family Time 3:

Leader Answers:

- Good
- Favor from the Lord

- What is good
- Discussion ideas: Favor is to be pleasing, acceptable to God, or to be approved by God. Isn't that our desire? We want to do what is right in God's eyes. Encourage each other to share things that are right and good that you can do as a family.

Family Time 4:

Leader Answers:

- Good news
- Good news
- The gospel
- Discussion ideas: Take turns struggling through saying the gospel. It can be awkward at first. Add to it your life before hearing the gospel and then the change after hearing it, and how God has worked in your life. Then you will have your testimony to the positive change Jesus brings in a life. Some of your family may not see a change in their lives. Encourage them to keep praying and asking Jesus to show Himself to them. For some the change is gradual, it is a process and everyone's pace is different; but it is important to note that you will see a good change if the belief in His Son, Jesus, is real.

Family Time 5:

Leader Answers:

- Perfect
- Perfect
- Walk in His statutes, observe His ordinances
- Discussion ideas: This can be moments when you know the right thing to do. Sometimes it is from another person's suggestion (a person God sent to talk to you) and you know the idea is right. When it comes from God it will not contradict His Word. If the idea does contradict God's Word, then the idea is not from God. It can be words of encouragement to another, a phone call, or email. It can be of service…helping the needy, making a meal.

MONTH 5

Directions:

As a group, either go through all five "family times" at one time or break it up over four-five weeks, depending on the month.

First – Talk with God

God speaks to you…read the passages and answer the questions.

Reading God's Word, the Holy Bible, is God's way of telling us how to live life. Give Him the time to speak to you. Read the passage first all the way through. Then go back and answer the questions.

Then – Walk with God

Walking…is the action of moving forward with God's instruction from your talk with Him.

And Pray – don't skip this part!

Praying…is your time to talk to God. Prayer is the system that God has designed for you to ask for God's help and you are able to ask because of your relationship with God's only begotten Son, Jesus Christ. If you want to walk with God and hear His direction for you, then you have to ask Him to help you.

For more family activities and devotional ideas to help bring your time in the Word to life, please visit the Sky Ranch Family Devo Resource page. There you will find supplemental activities for each section of the devotional.

www.skyranch.org/familydevoresource

Family Time 1:

Month 5 Topic: There is only one God…Recognizing the One True God

Talk with God: Read… Isaiah 44:6, Isaiah 45:21-22

> **Isaiah 44:6 Thus saith the LORD the King of Israel, and His redeemer the LORD of hosts; "I am the first, and I am the last; and beside Me there is no God."**

- In Isaiah 44:6, is there any other God besides the Lord?

> **Isaiah 45:21-22 Declare and set forth your case; indeed, let them consult together. Who has announced this from of old? Who has long since declared it? Is it not I, the Lord? And there is no other God besides Me, a righteous God and a Savior; there is none except Me. (22) Turn to Me and be saved, all the ends of the earth; for I am God, and there is no other.**

- In Isaiah 45:21-22, turn to whom to be saved?

Walk with God: Discuss…There is no other God. The Lord of hosts is God. He alone saves us. He is righteous. He is the first and the last. Have you ever wondered if there are other gods or if there is a God? Do you know someone who believes in a different god? What convinced you that the LORD of hosts is the only True God?

Prayer suggestion… Pray that you would recognize the One True God.

Family Time 2:

Month 5 Topic: There is only one God…God does not lie

Talk with God: Read…John 17:3, Isaiah 45:5, Titus 1:2

John 17:3 This is life eternal, that they might know You the only true God, and Jesus Christ, Whom You have sent.

- In John 17:3, what kind of God is our God called?

Isaiah 45:5 I am the Lord, and there is no other; besides Me there is no God. I will gird you, though you have not known Me; (6) that men may know from the rising to the setting of the sun that there is no One besides Me. I am the Lord, and there is no other, (7) the One forming light and creating darkness, causing well-being and creating calamity; I am the Lord who does all.

- In Isaiah 45:5, what kinds of things does our God do?

Titus 1:2 In the hope of eternal life, which God, Who cannot lie, promised long ages ago, these.

- In Titus 1:2, God can do everything but one thing, what?

Walk with God: Discuss… What is the opposite of TRUE? False! God is saying that He is truthful. And we see that God cannot lie about it. What is the witness that He is the only God?

Prayer suggestion… Pray that God will open your eyes to the One True God.

Family Time 3:

Month 5 Topic: There is only one God…Prophecy

Talk with God: Read… Jeremiah 10:10, Daniel 2:21-22, Acts 15:16-18

> **Jeremiah 10:10** But the Lord is the true God; He is the living God and the everlasting King. At His wrath the earth quakes and the nations cannot endure His indignation.

- In Jer 10:10, what kind of God is our God?

> **Daniel 2:21, 22** And it is He Who changes the times and the epochs; He removes kings and establishes kings; He gives wisdom to wise men, and knowledge to men of understanding. (22) It is He Who reveals the profound and hidden things; He knows what is in the darkness, and the light dwells with Him.

- In Dan 2:21, what does God change, establish, and give?

> **Acts 15:16-18** "After these things I will return, and I will rebuild the tabernacle of David which has fallen, and I will rebuild its ruins, and I will restore it, (17) in order that the rest of mankind may seek the Lord, and all the Gentiles who are called by My name," (18) says the Lord, Who makes these things known from of old.

- In Acts 15:18, when does God make things known from?

Walk with God: Discuss… God tells us that He is the only God by telling us things before they happen. This special knowledge is called prophecy. When we see prophecy like in Acts 15:16-18 actually happen, it is proof that God is Who He says He is. Discuss other prophecies that have been fulfilled. What prophecies can you think of that have been fulfilled?

Prayer suggestion… Pray that the Lord would help you understand His prophecy.

Family Time 4:

Month 5 Topic: There is only one God...Vain things

Talk with God: Read...Daniel 6:26, Acts 14:15

> **Daniel 6:26** **For He is the living God and enduring forever, and His Kingdom is one which will not be destroyed, and His dominion [will be] forever.**

- In Dan 6:26, what kind of God is our God?

> **Acts 14:15** **And saying, "Men, why are you doing these things. We are also men of the same nature as you, and preach the gospel to you in order that you should turn from these vain things to a living God, Who made the heaven and the earth and the sea, and all that is in them."**

- In Acts 14:15, what are we to turn from?

Walk with God: Discuss...The problem of trusting in "vain" things. What kinds of things are "vain" things? Vain things are anything that makes us excessively proud or puts the focus on us, rather than God. Are there vain things in your life? How do you turn away from them and turn back to the living God?

Prayer suggestion... Pray that the Lord will fill you up with so much of Him that there is no room left for "vain things"!

Family Time 5:

Month 5 Topic: There is only one God...Belief in God affects lifestyle

Talk with God: Read...Deuteronomy 4:35, Deuteronomy 4:39

> **Deuteronomy 4:35 To you it was shown that you might know that the Lord, He is God; there is no other besides Him.**

- In Deuteronomy 4:35, whom does the Lord want to know that there is no other god beside Him?

> **Deuteronomy 4:39 Know therefore today, and take it to your heart, that the Lord, He is God in Heaven above and on the earth below; there is no other.**

- In Deuteronomy 4:39, when do we need to trust that the God of Heaven and earth is the only God?

Walk with God: Discuss... Have you really taken it to your heart that there is only ONE God? How does your life reflect that in your everyday lifestyle? What are some things you can do to show that you KNOW HIM?

Prayer suggestion... Pray that you truly take to heart that you know and believe the One True God!

Leader Answers:

Month 5 Topic: There is only one God

Family Time 1:

Leader Answers:

- No
- God
- Discussion ideas: This is a difficult truth to explain to some-one at all, but even harder to explain to someone who does not regard God's Word, the Bible. Many religions make claims, but God tells us that Jesus is the Way to Him...the One True God. With tough subjects like this, always pray and ask for God's direction as the issue is discussed. Pray with your friend and ask God to show them...He will.

Family Time 2:

Leader Answers:

- Only True God
- Formed light, created darkness, causes well-being, creates calamity
- Lie
- Discussion ideas: God is sovereign over creation. Romans 1:20 says that God gives us creation as a witness that He alone is God. God's ability to cause things good or bad to happen is another witness that He alone is God. What else shows you He is God?

Family Time 3:

Leader Answers:

- True, living, everlasting
- Times, epochs; kings; wisdom/knowledge
- Things known from of old
- Discussion ideas: Many prophecies of Jesus were fulfilled when He arrived 2000 years ago. Look at (Jesus' birth) Isaiah 7:14, then Matthew 1:18-25. Look at (Jesus' death) Psalm 22:1-24, then Matthew 27:45-66. There are many more like these. Only prophecy from God is 100% accurate.

Family Time 4:

Leader Answers:

- Living, enduring
- Vain things
- Discussion ideas: Vain things can be anything we place above God such as clothes, precious items, a car, jewelry, money or a hobby, other people, TV, celebrities or vices, alcohol, gambling, or working too much at our job. It can be anything more important to you than God. If we are caught by these things, surrender back to God as Lord of your life and repent. Apologize.

Family Time 5:

Leader Answers:

- YOU
- Today
- Discussion ideas: Examples are spending time with Him (prayer), reading His Word, studying Him and making changes inside of you as to living the way He says. Other examples are serving Him by helping the needy, encouraging others, discipling another, talking about Him, donating to ministry, cleaning a yard for a homebound person, etc. How does it make you feel to know that the One True God wants to know and love you?

MONTH 6

Directions:

As a group, either go through all five "family times" at one time or break it up over four-five weeks, depending on the month.

First – Talk with God

God speaks to you...read the passages and answer the questions.

Reading God's Word, the Holy Bible, is God's way of telling us how to live life. Give Him the time to speak to you. Read the passage first all the way through. Then go back and answer the questions.

Then – Walk with God

Walking...is the action of moving forward with God's instruction from your talk with Him.

And Pray – don't skip this part!

Praying...is your time to talk to God. Prayer is the system that God has designed for you to ask for God's help and you are able to ask because of your relationship with God's only begotten Son, Jesus Christ. If you want to walk with God and hear His direction for you, then you have to ask Him to help you.

For more family activities and devotional ideas to help bring your time in the Word to life, please visit the Sky Ranch Family Devo Resource page. There you will find supplemental activities for each section of the devotional.

www.skyranch.org/familydevoresource

Family Time 1:

Month 6 Topic: God is love…Love changes us

Talk with God: Read…1 John 4:10, 1 John 4:8, 1 John 4:16

1 John 4:10 In this is love, not that we loved God, but that He loved us and sent His Son [to be] the propitiation for our sins. Beloved, if God so loved us, we also ought to love one another.

- In 1 John 4:10, what is love?

1 John 4:8 The one who does not love does not know God, for God is love.

- In 1 John 4:8, who is love?

1 John 4:16 And we have come to know and have believed the love which God has for us. God is love, and the one who abides in love abides in God, and God abides in him.

- In 1 John 4:16, how do I show others that I know God?

Walk with God: Discuss… The greatest love ever given was Jesus. How has that gift changed you?

Prayer suggestion… Thank God for loving you and sending Jesus as a payment for your sins.

Family Time 2:

Month 6 Topic: God is love...Seeing Jesus' love in you

Talk with God: Read...John 13:34, Galatians 5:22-23, Job 10:12

John 13:34 A new commandment I give to you, that you love one another, even as I have loved you, that you also love one another.

- In John 13:34, Jesus commands what?

Galatians 5:22-23 But the fruit of the Spirit is love, joy, peace, patience, kindness, goodness, faithfulness, gentleness, self-control; against such things there is no law.

- In Gal 5:22-23, someone who is guided by the Spirit will _____ others.

Job 10:12 You have granted me life and loving-kindness; and Your care has preserved my spirit.

- In Job 10:12, what has God given to us?

Walk with God: Discuss... How do others see God's love through you? Discuss ideas and practical ways you can show God's love to others.

Prayer suggestion... Ask God to bring to your mind someone that needs love.

Family Time 3:

Month 6 Topic: God is love…Love like God loves

Talk with God: Read…Exodus 34:6, 1 Chronicles 16:34, Psalm 36:7

Exodus 34:6 The Lord, the Lord God, compassionate and gracious, slow to anger, and abounding in loving-kindness and truth; Who keeps loving-kindness for thousands, who forgives iniquity, transgression and sin.

- In Ex 34:6, how much loving-kindness does God have?

1 Chronicles 16:34 O give thanks to the Lord, for [He is] good; for His loving-kindness is everlasting.

- In 1 Chr 16:34, when will His loving-kindness end?

Psalm 36:7 How precious is Your loving-kindness, O God! And the children of men take refuge in the shadow of Your wings.

- In Ps 36:7, because of His loving-kindness, we can do what?

Walk with God: Discuss… Can you love like God loves? We are to imitate Him. We can probably be compassionate and gracious at times. But are you slow to anger? Anger can be a challenge for all of us. I am very glad God is slow to anger, are you? Do you show that same kindness to others? What are some ways to help slow your anger down and show the mercy that God shows?

Prayer suggestion… Thank Him for loving you with His endless love! Ask Him to increase your ability to love others as He loves you.

Family Time 4:

Month 6 Topic: God is love...Showing God's love through obedience

Talk with God: Read...1 John 4:19, John 14:15, 2 Chronicles 6:14

1 John 4:19 We love, because He first loved us.

- In 1 John 4:19, who initiated love?

John 14:15 If you love Me, you will keep My commandments.

- In John 14:15, if I love God, what will I do?

2 Chronicles 6:14 And he said, "O Lord, the God of Israel, there is no god like You in Heaven or on earth, keeping covenant and [showing] loving-kindness to Your servants who walk before You with all their heart."

- In 2 Chr 6:14, who does God show loving-kindness toward?

Walk with God: Discuss... Love is an action. The best way we can show God we love Him is by being obedient to Him. Are there areas of our lives that we need to change to be more obedient? The shows we watch? The music we listen to? The friends we hang out with?

Prayer suggestion... Ask God to show you your areas of disobedience and for His help in making changes in your life that show Him you love Him.

Family Time 5:

Month 6 Topic: God is love…God's love/parent's love

Talk with God: Read…Romans 8:38, Psalm 136:1

> **Romans 8:38** For I am convinced that neither death, nor life, nor angels, nor principalities, nor things present, nor things to come, nor powers, nor height, nor depth, nor any other created thing, shall be able to separate us from the love of God, which is in Christ Jesus our Lord.

- In Rom 8:38, what can separate me from God's love?

> **Psalm 136:1** Give thanks to the Lord, for He is good; for His loving-kindness is everlasting.

- In Ps 136:1, how do I respond to His everlasting kindness?

Walk with God: Discuss… How does it make you feel to know that God will NEVER stop loving you? Pretty awesome! Parents are to imitate God's parenting style and love our children the way that God loves us. Discuss the parent/child role and how as a parent no matter what the child ever does…your love will NEVER change.

Prayer suggestion… Thank Him for His power and everlasting loving-kindness.

Leader Answers:

Month 6 Topic: God is love

Family Time 1:
Leader Answers:
- He loved us and sent His Son to pay for our sins
- God
- Abide in love = love
- Discussion ideas: God's love changes us from the inside out. Hearts that were hardened become soft. God's Holy Spirit lives in us and causes us to treat others in the way that we want to be treated. Examples are kindness, gentleness, truthfulness, encouragement, etc., and we stop being greedy, hurtful, mean, outbursts of anger, etc.

Family Time 2:
Leader Answers:
- Love one another
- Love
- Life and loving-kindness
- Discussion ideas: We often think of the obvious things like feed or shelter the needy or give money to or care for someone who is hurt, build someone up by encouraging. But what about the less obvious things like a wife who doesn't say that mean, nagging thing to her husband, or a husband who doesn't criticize his wife's housekeeping style? Love can be shown in the things we refrain from saying, too. Any other ideas?

Family Time 3:
Leader Answers:
- It is abounding
- Never
- Take shelter in Him
- Discussion ideas: Anger is tough. Anger is the result of feeling that you have been treated unjustly. A common response to anger

is revenge, but God tells us that we are not to seek revenge; vengeance is His (Romans 12:19). Examples of handling anger correctly are pray, make sure you know the facts correctly, talk calmly to each other. Matthew 18:15 defines a Biblical way to handle disputes, forgive and show mercy.

Family Time 4:

Leader Answers:

- God
- Obey and keep His commandments
- Servants who walk uprightly before Him with all their heart
- Discussion ideas: Obedience is keeping God's Word. But you have to know it to be obedient to it. Do you know it? Could you know it better?

Family Time 5:

Leader Answers:

- Nothing
- Give thanks
- Discussion ideas: God loves us. Parents love their children. God has placed an instinctive love in a parent for their offspring that is unique. It is called "philoteknos" (love in Greek in Titus 2:4) and this love gives parents a desire to meet their child's needs. We also are to show "agape" (love in Greek in John 3:35) and this love desires the highest good for the child, even if they have done something wrong. Hug your kids and tell them you love them!

MONTH 7

Directions:
As a group, either go through all five "family times" at one time or
break it up over four-five weeks, depending on the month.

First – Talk with God

God speaks to you…read the passages and answer the questions.

Reading God's Word, the Holy Bible, is God's way of telling us
how to live life. Give Him the time to speak to you. Read the
passage first all the way through. Then go back and answer the
questions.

Then – Walk with God

Walking…is the action of moving forward with God's instruction
from your talk with Him.

And Pray – don't skip this part!

Praying…is your time to talk to God. Prayer is the system that
God has designed for you to ask for God's help and you are able
to ask because of your relationship with God's only begotten Son,
Jesus Christ. If you want to walk with God and hear His direction for you, then you have to ask Him to help you.

For more family activities and devotional ideas to help bring your
time in the Word to life, please visit the Sky Ranch Family Devo
Resource page. There you will find supplemental activities for each
section of the devotional.

www.skyranch.org/familydevoresource

Family Time 1:

Month 7 Topic: God works to preserve and rule all of creation...
Preserve God's covenants/commands

Talk with God: Read...Nehemiah 1:5, Psalm 97:10, Proverbs 2:8

Nehemiah 1:5 O Lord God of Heaven, the great and awesome God, Who preserves the covenant and loving-kindness for those who love Him and keep His commandments.

- In Neh 1:5, who is God preserving the covenant and loving-kindness for?

Psalm 97:10 Hate evil, you who love the Lord, Who preserves the souls of His godly ones; He delivers them from the hand of the wicked.

- In Ps 97:10, whose souls are preserved?

Proverbs 2:8 Guarding the paths of justice, and He preserves the way of His godly ones.

- In Prov 2:8, what does He preserve of the godly ones?

Walk with God: Discuss... In this passage, preserving is to guard, keep watch or ward, to protect. God preserves those who love Him and keep His commandments, their souls, and their way. Do you want this protection from God? Are you considered one of His godly ones? How do you know?

Prayer suggestion... Pray that the Lord would help you love Him and keep His commandments (teachings).

Family Time 2:

Month 7 Topic: God works to preserve and rule all of creation... Worship

Talk with God: Read...Nehemiah 9:6, Hebrews 1:3

> **Nehemiah 9:6 You alone are the Lord; You have made the heavens, the Heaven of heavens, with all their host, the earth, and all that is on it, the seas, and all that is in them, and You give life to them all; and the host of Heaven bow down before You.**

- In Neh 9:6, God alone made all things. What is He doing for them?

> **Hebrews 1:3 (About Jesus)...And He is the radiance of His glory and the exact representation of His nature, and upholds all things by the Word of His power.**

- In Heb 1:3, what is God upholding by His power?

Walk with God: Discuss... The powerful God that created the world is the same God that lives in us. He can create the world and forgives our sins. No sin is too big to forgive for the Creator of the universe. Have you asked God to forgive you? Do you worship God for forgiving you? All the host of Heaven bow before Him (worship Him). What does worship look like to you? What do you think the host of heaven worship looks like?

Prayer suggestion... God made Heaven and earth but He also made YOU. The Bible says if you do not praise Him, the rocks will cry out. Pray that you will praise Him for all He has done.

Family Time 3:

Month 7 Topic: God works to preserve and rule all of creation...
Allowing Him to be sovereign

Talk with God: Read...1 Timothy 6:15

1 Timothy 6:15 He Who is the blessed and only Sovereign, the King of kings and Lord of lords; (16) Who alone possesses immortality and dwells in unapproachable light; Whom no man has seen or can see.

- In 1 Tim 6:15, God is the King of kings and Lord of lords. He is blessed and what?

- In 1 Tim 6:15, what does God alone possess?

- (Isn't this cool?) In 1 Tim 6:15, where does God dwell?

Walk with God: Discuss... Is there anything that you try to be "sovereign" over? Usually it is our own lives. We like to control what we do and sometimes control others around us. But can two be the boss? Does it ever work out well? What does it mean to let God be sovereign over you? How do we recognize God's sovereignty in everyday life?

Prayer suggestion... Pray for God to help your family allow the Sovereign God to rule in your lives.

Family Time 4:

Month 7 Topic: God works to preserve and rule all of creation…His power/leading…imitation

Talk with God: Read…2 Chronicles 20:6, Daniel 5:21

> **2 Chronicles 20:6 And he said, "O Lord, the God of our fathers, are You not God in the heavens? And are You not ruler over all the kingdoms of the nations? Power and might are in Your hand so that no one can stand against You."**

- In 2 Chr 20:6, who is ruler over all the kingdoms of nations?

> **Daniel 5:21 He recognized that the Most High God is Ruler over the realm of mankind, and [that] He sets over it whomever He wishes.**

- In Dan 5:21, who puts rulers in place?

- In Dan 5:21, whom does God choose?

Walk with God: Discuss…Even though God is an all-powerful ruler, He still gives us the choice to follow Him in our lives. Are you a leader? Has God set you "over" something? What kind of ruler/leader are you?

Prayer suggestion… Pray for our country and the leaders God has put in place. Pray that you are a godly leader in your area of influence.

Family Time 5:

Month 7 Topic: God works to preserve and rule all of creation...
Our overall good

Talk with God: Read...Romans 8:28

> **Romans 8:28 And we know that God causes all things to work together for good to those who love God, to those who are called according to [His] purpose.**

- In Rom 8:28, what does God cause all things to work together for?

- In Rom 8:28, who is the group that He causes good for?

- In Rom 8:28, what is this group called for?

Walk with God: Discuss... Is there a time that you did not think something worked out the way you wanted, but you later realized it was really for your good? Share that time with each other...and the good result.

Prayer suggestion... Pray that you would see God working things "for your good" and not just wanting "good things."

Leader Answers:

Month 7 Topic: God works to preserve and rule all of creation

Family Time 1:

Leader Answers:

- Those who love Him
- His godly ones
- Their way
- Discussion ideas: This is a question that goes through everyone's mind. How do I know? Do you love God, His Son Jesus, His commandments (or teachings)? Do you follow Him in your lifestyle? Is it evident to you and others, too? You know your heart… if there is a doubt, pray, take it to God directly. He will show you in His timing. Earnestly seek Him and you will find Him (Deuteronomy 4:29).

Family Time 2:

Leader Answers:

- He gives life to them all
- All things
- Discussion ideas: God, the Creator, designed the world and a way of life that we are to follow. When we do not follow His way of life, and create our own way, we offend Him and this offense separates us from Him. We stay separated until we ask for forgiveness and change to follow His way. The way of life is laid out for us in the Bible, His Scripture. We worship because we are thankful for His forgiveness. Worship can look like singing praises out loud or in your heart, praying, serving, anything that praises Him.

Family Time 3:

Leader Answers:

- Sovereign
- Immortality
- In unapproachable light

- Discussion ideas: When God is sovereign over your life it means that He has the authority over your life or lifestyle. God does not contradict Himself, meaning He won't contradict His Word. Scripture is your guide as well as God's Holy Spirit, too. It is living life according to the way the Bible tells us to live. That is why Jesus said, "If you love me, you will obey my commands" (John 14:15). Examples are your love of God/Jesus, your treatment of others, your service to others, your love for others. Do you seek God first (Matthew 6:33)?

Family Time 4:

Leader Answers:
- God
- God
- Whomever He wishes
- Discussion ideas: Jesus was a servant leader. He led by example. We can do the same. Study His leadership style. Discuss how you handle a leader that you don't agree with. How do you handle a leader that God has appointed and then leads contrary to God's Word? Pray. There is a lot of power in prayer. Read in Scripture how Jesus handled it.

Family Time 5:

Leader Answers:
- Good
- Those who love God
- His purposes
- Discussion ideas: We have to trust that God has the big picture of "our good" in mind and that His Kingdom purpose is always more important than what we want all the time. Examples could be a friendship ended, a job lost, a sickness…but a blessing resulted such as the friend was making bad choices in life, the new job found was better for you, the sickness ended and taught you to value your health.

MONTH 8

Directions:

As a group, either go through all five "family times" at one time or break it up over four-five weeks, depending on the month.

First – Talk with God

God speaks to you…read the passages and answer the questions.

Reading God's Word, the Holy Bible, is God's way of telling us how to live life. Give Him the time to speak to you. Read the passage first all the way through. Then go back and answer the questions.

Then – Walk with God

Walking…is the action of moving forward with God's instruction from your talk with Him.

And Pray – don't skip this part!

Praying…is your time to talk to God. Prayer is the system that God has designed for you to ask for God's help and you are able to ask because of your relationship with God's only begotten Son, Jesus Christ. If you want to walk with God and hear His direction for you, then you have to ask Him to help you.

For more family activities and devotional ideas to help bring your time in the Word to life, please visit the Sky Ranch Family Devo Resource page. There you will find supplemental activities for each section of the devotional.

www.skyranch.org/familydevoresource

Family Time 1:

Month 8 Topic: God is my Heavenly Father Who guides and cares for me…We are adopted

Talk with God: Read…Matthew 6:9, Romans 8:15

Matthew 6:9 Our Father, who is in Heaven, hallowed be Your name.

- In Matthew 6:9, what type of Father is God?

Romans 8:15 For you have not received a spirit of slavery leading to fear again, but you have received a spirit of adoption as sons by which we cry out, "Abba! Father!"

- In Romans 8:15, why can I call Him "Daddy" or "Father"?

Walk with God: Discuss…the adoption process for choosing a child from an orphanage to a loving home. The Lord loves us so much He has chosen us to be with Him as His child forever. He wants you to be a part of His family. You are part of a large family. How does that affect your view of God, knowing that He has adopted you? How about your view of other Christians?

Prayer suggestion… Pray for God to help us understand the magnitude of His caring for us, and thank Him for choosing us to be a part of His family.

Family Time 2:

Month 8 Topic: God is my Heavenly Father Who guides and cares for me…Shepherd that leads

Talk with God: Read…Psalm 23:1-3

> **Psalm 23:1-3 (A Psalm of David) The Lord is my Shepherd, I shall not want. (2) He makes me lie down in green pastures; He leads me beside quiet waters. (3) He restores my soul; He guides me in the paths of righteousness For His Name's sake.**

- In Ps 23:1-3, what does God do?

Walk with God: Discuss… Who is a shepherd?
  A. A pastor is a shepherd to the church.
  B. An elder or deacon is a shepherd within the body.
  C. A husband is a shepherd to his wife.
  D. Parents are shepherds to their children.
  E. A teacher is a shepherd to his students.
  F. An employer is a shepherd to his employees.
  G. An older child is a shepherd to his younger brothers and sisters.
  H. Anyone who in any way leads anyone is a shepherd who is responsible for the care of another.

Prayer suggestion… Pray that the Lord show you who your sheep are and how you are a shepherd. Ask the Lord to show you who you can shepherd.

Family Time 3:

Month 8 Topic: God is my Heavenly Father Who guides and cares for me…Shepherd that cares for us

Talk with God: Read…Psalm 100:3-4

> **Psalm 100:3-4 Know that the Lord Himself is God; it is He Who has made us, and not we ourselves; we are His people and the sheep of His pasture. (4) Enter His gates with thanksgiving and His courts with praise. Give thanks to Him, bless His name.**

- According to this Scripture, what should our response be?

Walk with God: Discuss… How does a shepherd care for his sheep, and how are we the sheep of the Lord's pasture?

He is The Almighty Shepherd.

Discuss what the shepherd does for the sheep.
1. A good shepherd gives the sheep a sense of belonging.
2. The shepherd should see that the needs of the sheep are met.
3. The shepherd should not be a slave driver, but one who provides rest and guidance and leads his sheep.

Prayer suggestion… Pray a prayer of thanksgiving that the Lord will guide and protect you. Then pray a prayer of praise that He has done so.

Family Time 4:

Month 8 Topic: God is my Heavenly Father Who guides and cares for me...Daily guide

Talk with God: Read...Psalm 31:3, Proverbs 6:20-22

> **Psalm 31:3   For You are my rock and my fortress; for Your name's sake You will lead me and guide me.**

- In Ps 31:3, what will God do?

> **Proverbs 6:20-22 (20) My son, observe the commandment of your father, and do not forsake the teaching of your mother; (21) bind them continually on your heart; tie them around your neck. (22) When you walk about, they will guide you; when you sleep, they will watch over you; and when you awake, they will talk to you.**

- In Prov 6:20-22, what has been given to us as a daily guide in life?

Walk with God: Discuss... What do we as believers have to help us and guide us? How does God's Word help us? Give examples from Scripture that have helped guide you.

Prayer suggestion... Pray for you to decrease so He can increase and be your guide. Pray that you will move out of the way and totally rely on Him for guidance in your life.

Family Time 5:

Month 8 Topic: God is my Heavenly Father Who guides and cares for me...Dealing with anxiety/worry

Talk with God: Read...1 Pet 5:7

> **1 Pet 5:7 Casting all your anxiety upon Him, because He cares for you.**

- In 1 Pet 5:7, God tells us to give Him our worries. Why?

Walk with God: Discuss... Do you worry or have anxious feelings? How do you typically handle your worry/anxiety for school, work, finances, friends, etc? What are we supposed to do in these situations? Why are we to totally cast all anxiety on Him?

Prayer suggestion... Pray that you will cast all your worry and anxiety over everything to the Lord.

Leader Answers:

Family Time 1:

Month 8 Topic: God is my Heavenly Father Who guides and cares for me

Leader Answers:

- Holy, Heavenly
- He has adopted me, given me His Spirit
- Discussion ideas: Adoption may be tough for younger members in the family to understand. Explain that Mom and Dad love their adopted kids very much. God loves each of us very much, too. Also, discuss how we are to love other Christians. Let the group discuss their response to other Christians. It can be tough to show that love, especially in the church parking lot! Or if there is division instead of unity among Christians.

Family Time 2:

Leader Answers:

- Provides rest, food, water; restores; guides rightly
- Discussion ideas: All are a form of a shepherd. Use these examples to discuss how you have been shepherded or shepherded someone else.

Family Time 3:

Leader Answers:

- Thanks, praise, blessing
- Discussion ideas: God cares for us. We can see it in many forms. In our physical needs of food, water, shelter, clothing. But what about our spiritual needs, emotional needs, companion needs, etc.? Discuss the less obvious ways that you have seen God's care.

Family Time 4:

Leader Answers:

- Lead; guide
- Commandments (His Word); teaching
- Discussion ideas: How about Exodus 20, the Ten Commandments? The Book of Proverbs tells about questionable people to watch out for. Revelation 1-3 divides the real Christian from the fake Christian. There is insight to guide us in every book of the Bible.

Family Time 5:

Leader Answers:

- Because He cares for you
- Discussion ideas: Most people typically don't think to turn to God first to deal with their anxiety or worry. Where do people typically turn? Other people, or they try to avoid thinking about it by using distractions: TV, shopping, eating, alcohol, etc. But God says cast these anxieties on Him. How do you do that? Pray. Give it all to Him. Ask Him to help you. Then, after prayer, it is okay to seek wise counsel from people. God can send people to help us. Just ask Him about it first.

MONTH 9

Directions:

As a group, either go through all five "family times" at one time or break it up over four-five weeks, depending on the month.

First – Talk with God

God speaks to you…read the passages and answer the questions.

Reading God's Word, the Holy Bible, is God's way of telling us how to live life. Give Him the time to speak to you. Read the passage first all the way through. Then go back and answer the questions.

Then – Walk with God

Walking…is the action of moving forward with God's instruction from your talk with Him.

And Pray – don't skip this part!

Praying…is your time to talk to God. Prayer is the system that God has designed for you to ask for God's help and you are able to ask because of your relationship with God's only begotten Son, Jesus Christ. If you want to walk with God and hear His direction for you, then you have to ask Him to help you.

For more family activities and devotional ideas to help bring your time in the Word to life, please visit the Sky Ranch Family Devo Resource page. There you will find supplemental activities for each section of the devotional.

www.skyranch.org/familydevoresource

Family Time 1:

Month 9 Topic: God is my King and my purpose...Understanding Kingship

Talk with God: Read...Matthew 6:10, Psalm 19:14, Ephesians 2:10

Matthew 6:10 Your Kingdom come, Your will be done on earth as it is in Heaven.

- Whose will did Jesus pray for in Matt 6:10?

Psalm 19:14 Let the words of my mouth, and the meditation of my heart, be acceptable in Your sight, O LORD, my strength, and my redeemer.

- Whose acceptance are we looking for in Psalm 19:14?

Ephesians 2:10 For we are His workmanship, created in Christ Jesus for good works, which God prepared beforehand, that we should walk in them.

- In Eph 2:10, who are we and why were we created?

Walk with God: Discuss... Is it hard to recognize God as our King? Why? How should our lives be a reflection of Him as King? Should the life we live (i.e., our works) be representative of Him? How can we do this on a daily basis?

Prayer suggestion... Ask God to reveal His will to your family so that you can move forward with Him.

Family Time 2:

Month 9 Topic: God is my King and my purpose...Obedience to the King

Talk with God: Read...Psalm 119:1-6 (NLT)

1 Joyful are people of integrity,
  who follow the instructions of the Lord.

2 Joyful are those who obey his laws
  and search for Him with all their hearts.

- What brings us joy?

3 They do not compromise with evil,
  and they walk only in His paths.

4 You have charged us
  to keep Your commandments carefully.

- How are we to keep His commandments?

5 Oh, that my actions would consistently
  reflect Your decrees!

6 Then I will not be ashamed
  when I compare my life with Your commands.

- According to v5, what should our actions reflect?

Walk with God: Discuss... If God is our King, then we should obey Him, right? Why is this so hard? Would it be easier to obey an earthly king? Why?

Prayer suggestion... Ask God to remind your family on a daily basis that He is King. He is on His throne and He is Lord!

Family Time 3:

Month 9 Topic: God is my King and my purpose...Service to the King

Talk with God: Read...Romans 12:1, 6-8

> **Romans 12:1** Therefore I urge you dear brothers to offer your bodies as living sacrifices, holy and pleasing to God – this is your spiritual act of worship. Do not conform any longer to the patterns of this world but be transformed by the renewing of your mind. Then you will be able to test and approve what God's will is – His good, pleasing and perfect will.

- What do we need to do first, before we test and approve God's will, according to v1?

- Is God's will perfect in v1?

> **Romans 12:6-8** And since we have gifts that differ according to the grace given to us, let each exercise them accordingly; if prophecy, according to the proportion of his faith; (7) if service, in his serving, or he who teaches, in his teaching; (8) or he who exhorts, in his exhortation; he who gives, with liberality; he who leads, with diligence; he who shows mercy, with cheerfulness.

- Why do we all have different gifts per v6-8?

Walk with God: Discuss... As we just read, all members of the body have different gifts. What gifts is your family blessed with? Go around and discuss these gifts as a family. How can you serve others with these gifts? Are you using them for the Lord? Why or why not? Set goals to begin using your gifts as a family to serve and minister to those around you.

Prayer suggestion... Ask God to help you use your gifts as a family for His glory.

Family Time 4:

Month 9 Topic: God is my King and my purpose...Sing praises to the King

Talk with God: Read...Psalm 100:1-5

> **Psalm 100:1-5 Shout joyfully to the Lord, all the earth. (2) Serve the Lord with gladness; come before Him with joyful singing.**

- How are we to serve the Lord according to v100:2?

> **(3) Know that the Lord Himself is God; it is He Who has made us, and not we ourselves; we are His people and the sheep of His pasture.**

> **(4) Enter His gates with thanksgiving and His courts with praise. Give thanks to Him; bless His name.**

> **(5) For the Lord is good; His loving-kindness is everlasting, and His faithfulness to all generations.**

- In Ps 100:5, is the Lord good? How do you know?
- What else is the Lord, per Ps 100:5?

Walk with God: Discuss... The Psalms are also songs. In fact, you could "sing" the Scripture above if you wanted to! Remember, David was quite an accomplished harpist. Sing together as a family a hymn or spiritual song, such as "Great is Thy Faithfulness" or "Holy, Holy, Holy." Singing praises to God is an act of worship. He covets the praises of His people.

Prayer suggestion... Pray for a heart full of thanksgiving and praise.

Family Time 5:

Month 9 Topic: God is my King and my purpose...Serving others for Him

Talk with God: Read...1 Timothy 1:12, Hebrews 12:28, 1 Corinthians 8:6

> **1 Timothy 1:12 I thank Christ Jesus our Lord, Who has strengthened me, because He considered me faithful, putting me into service.**

- According to 1 Tim 1:12, who strengthens us so we can serve?

> **Hebrews 12:28 Therefore, since we receive a Kingdom which cannot be shaken, let us show gratitude, by which we may offer to God an acceptable service with reverence and awe; for our God is a consuming fire.**

- In Heb 12:28, what are we to show as we serve?

> **1 Corinthians 8:6 Yet for us there is but one God, the Father, from Whom are all things, and we exist for Him; and one Lord, Jesus Christ, by Whom are all things, and we exist through Him.**

- Why do we exist per 1 Cor. 8:6? Does this change your perspective?

Walk with God: Discuss... Have all family members take a piece of paper and list who and how they served this week. Maybe as a family member, or a friend at school, or a co-worker. If God is our purpose and He is our King, then when we serve others, aren't we serving Him? We exist for Him and through Him. Discuss changes your family can make on a daily basis to better reflect your purpose in life.

Prayer suggestion... Ask God to remove the things in your lives that take preeminence over Him.

Leader Answers:

Family Time 1:

Month 9 Topic: God is my King and my purpose
Leader Answers:

- God's will
- The Lord's
- God's workmanship; for good works
- Discussion ideas: It's hard sometimes to recognize Him as King because we can't physically see Him like we might see an earthly king. Spending time with Him, worshipping Him and being obedient makes the relationship more real.

Family Time 2:

Leader Answers:

- Integrity and obedience
- Carefully
- His decrees (His Words)
- Discussion ideas: Obedience to God is sometimes hard because it is OUR decision. Sometimes no one but God knows when we are disobedient. That's when character counts!

Family Time 3:

Leader Answers:

- Offer our bodies as living sacrifices, holy and pleasing to God
- Yes
- We have different gifts so we can all serve in different ways, meeting the needs of the body of Christ
- Discussion ideas: Don't limit yourselves to the gifts written in these verses. Many gifts are given to God's people. Some will be easy to state, yet others will be more introspective and

thoughtful. Bless each family member and exhort through this time.

Family Time 4:

Leader Answers:

- With gladness
- Yes, His Word says so (Psalm 100:5) and He created us for a relationship with Him. He loves us and is good.
- His loving-kindness is everlasting and His faithfulness is to all generations
- Discussion ideas: This can be a wonderful time as a family to sing a hymn together and praise the Lord. Don't worry about sounding beautiful! The Lord knows your heart!

Family Time 5:

Leader Answers:

- Jesus Christ our Lord
- Gratitude
- We exist for God the Father. (Sometimes we think we exist for ourselves or this earth or our family.)
- Discussion ideas: Serving others is THE way we serve God. We are to be His hands and His feet. A family that serves together, grows in the Lord together.

MONTH 10

Directions:

As a group, either go through all five "family times" at one time or break it up over four-five weeks, depending on the month.

First – Talk with God

God speaks to you…read the passages and answer the questions.

Reading God's Word, the Holy Bible, is God's way of telling us how to live life. Give Him the time to speak to you. Read the passage first all the way through. Then go back and answer the questions.

Then – Walk with God

Walking…is the action of moving forward with God's instruction from your talk with Him.

And Pray – don't skip this part!

Praying…is your time to talk to God. Prayer is the system that God has designed for you to ask for God's help and you are able to ask because of your relationship with God's only begotten Son, Jesus Christ. If you want to walk with God and hear His direction for you, then you have to ask Him to help you.

For more family activities and devotional ideas to help bring your time in the Word to life, please visit the Sky Ranch Family Devo Resource page. There you will find supplemental activities for each section of the devotional.

www.skyranch.org/familydevoresource

OPEN YOUR EYES

Family Time 1:

Month 10 Topic: God is my Provider... God provides

Talk with God: Read...Matthew 6:11-12 and Philippians 4:11, 19

> **Matthew 6:11-12 Give us this day our daily bread. Forgive us our debts as we forgive our debtors. And lead us not into temptation, but deliver us from evil.**

- Jesus was modeling a prayer for us in Matthew 6:11-12. In these verses, what does He ask of God?

> **Philippians 4:11, 19 Not that I speak from want; for I have learned to be content in whatever circumstances I am...And my God will supply all your need according to His riches in glory in Christ Jesus.**

- Philippians 4:11, 19 shows us that Christ is all we need. Who supplies all of our needs according to this verse? What does this verse say about our "wants"?

Walk with God: Discuss... Have each family member share, one at a time, one thing that God has provided for them today. For instance, lunch, air, clothes, etc. Go around your circle and see how long you can play this "game" of telling each other what God has done for you today. Then, discuss for a bit the needs in your life that God has not provided. Anything? Remember...wants and needs are very different!

Prayer suggestion... Share in a prayer of thanksgiving and praise for ALL God has done in your family's life today. He is your Provider.

Family Time 2:

Month 10 Topic: God is my Provider…God's security

Talk with God: Read…Job 24:23, Philippians 4:19

> **Job 24:23 He provides them with security, and they are supported; and His eyes are on their ways.**

- What does God provide to His people in Job 24:23?

- Where are His eyes in Job 24:23?

> **Philippians 4:19 And my God shall supply all your needs according to His riches in glory in Christ Jesus.**

- In Phil 4:19, what shall God supply? Whose riches are they?

Walk with God: Discuss… Does your family have a security system? Is it monitored by the police department or a security firm? Discuss how this makes you feel as a family. Secure? That same security is found in God. He provides this free of charge. Is anyone feeling anxious or in need? Are there family members who need prayer right now for a certain situation they are dealing with?

Prayer suggestion… Pray for your family. Pray that they feel the security that the Father provides if we only ask. He is our Creator, our Provider, and He knows our needs.

Family Time 3:

Month 10 Topic: God is my Provider...Giving

Talk with God: Read...Matthew 7:11, Genesis 22:14

Matthew 7:11 **If you then, being evil, know how to give good gifts to your children, how much more shall your Father who is in Heaven give what is good to those who ask Him!"**

- Who is evil, according to Matt 7:11?

- In Matt 7:11, how do we receive good gifts from our Father?

Genesis 22:14 **And Abraham called the name of that place "The Lord Will Provide," as it is said to this day, "In the mount of the Lord it will be provided."**

- In Gen 22:14, who named the place of provision "The Lord Will Provide"?

Walk with God: Discuss... Do you consider yourself evil? What do you think God meant by this term? Parents, discuss the joy you feel when you give your children gifts. Kids, how do you feel to receive them? It's been said that Heaven is full of gifts (remember, yesterday's Scripture said Christ Jesus has riches!) just waiting to be bestowed upon us! Do we boldly go before God and ask for the desires of our heart? Sometimes all we need to do is ask. What have you asked God for lately, and has He answered your prayer?

Prayer suggestion... Thank God for providing for your needs. Thank Him for allowing you to provide for your family.

Family Time 4:

Month 10 Topic: God is my Provider...Needs

Talk with God: Read...Nehemiah 9:15, Nehemiah 9:21

> **Nehemiah 9:15 You provided bread from Heaven for them for their hunger, You brought forth water from a rock for their thirst.**

- In v15, what did God provide? Where did the water come from?

> **Nehemiah 9:21 Indeed, forty years You provided for them in the wilderness and they were not in want; their clothes did not wear out, nor did their feet swell.**

- In v21, how long did God provide for them in the wilderness? Were they in want? Did their clothes wear out? Did their feet swell?

Walk with God: Discuss... These verses remind us of how great God is and that He truly does supply all of our needs. Who among you has clothes you have worn for 40 years? Probably no one in your family still wears clothes that are 40 years old. When God provides, He really provides! Why is it important to thank God for our food prior to eating a meal? Recommit to doing this as a family before each meal. It will make mealtime much more enjoyable!

Prayer suggestion... "God, thank you for new clothes! And every meal we eat on a daily basis. Thank you for meeting our most basic needs like food, water and clothing."

Family Time 5:

Month 10 Topic: God is my Provider...Freedom from temptation

Talk with God: Read...1 Corinthians 10:13

1 Corinthians 10:13 **No temptation has overtaken you but such as is common to man; and God is faithful, Who will not allow you to be tempted beyond what you are able, but with the temptation will provide the way of escape also, that you may be able to endure it.**

- According to this Scripture, will God allow you to be tempted beyond what you are able to endure?

- Will He always provide a way of escape?

Walk with God: Discuss...Temptation is a scary thing sometimes. We don't know when it will rear its ugly head next. Jesus was tempted. He knows how we feel when we are tempted. He escaped the temptation and so can we, according to this verse. Why is it hard to escape? Is it sometimes easier to give in to the temptation? What have you been tempted with this week, today, in the last hour?

Prayer suggestion... Thank God for providing everything in your life. Thank Him for providing a way out of temptation and for making your family stronger through temptation.

Leader Answers:

Family Time 1:

Month 10 Topic: God is my Provider
Leader Answers:
- Daily bread, forgiveness and a way out of temptation
- God; be content in any circumstance
- Discussion ideas: You could probably go around listing God's provision for hours! Does defining needs and wants help you discern between your needs and wants?

Family Time 2:

Leader Answers:
- Security
- On their ways
- All your needs; Christ's riches
- Discussion ideas: Security is important for peace of mind. We sleep better knowing we are secure. If a family member is dealing with insecurity in a specific area, really listen and discuss, then pray for God's provision in this area.

Family Time 3:

Leader Answers:
- We are evil! (sinners)
- Ask
- Abraham
- Discussion ideas: Evildoers are sinners who are preoccupied with doing evil/wrong. We are all sinners and we still have redeeming qualities.

Family Time 4:

Leader Answers:

- Bread and water; from a rock
- 40 years; no; no; no
- Discussion ideas: Mealtime prayers are a great way to bring community to your family. Encourage your little ones to bow their heads to pray, even when they are not with you or at home. Prayers can be silent, but giving thanks is important.

Family Time 5:

Leader Answers:

- No
- Yes
- Discussion ideas: Matthew 4 tells the story of Jesus' temptation by Satan. This might be a good chapter to read to discuss temptation. Notice that Jesus counters Satan with Scripture...that works for us, too!

MONTH 11

Directions:
As a group, either go through all five "family times" at one time or break it up over four-five weeks, depending on the month.

First – Talk with God

God speaks to you…read the passages and answer the questions.

Reading God's Word, the Holy Bible, is God's way of telling us how to live life. Give Him the time to speak to you. Read the passage first all the way through. Then go back and answer the questions.

Then – Walk with God

Walking…is the action of moving forward with God's instruction from your talk with Him.

And Pray – don't skip this part!

Praying…is your time to talk to God. Prayer is the system that God has designed for you to ask for God's help and you are able to ask because of your relationship with God's only begotten Son, Jesus Christ. If you want to walk with God and hear His direction for you, then you have to ask Him to help you.

For more family activities and devotional ideas to help bring your time in the Word to life, please visit the Sky Ranch Family Devo Resource page. There you will find supplemental activities for each section of the devotional.

www.skyranch.org/familydevoresource

Family Time 1:

Month 11 Topic: God saves us...Receiving grace

Talk with God: Read...Isaiah 45:22, Ephesians 2:8-9

Isaiah 45:22 Turn to Me, and be saved, all the ends of the earth; for I am God, and there is no other.

- In Isaiah 45:22, what does God claim to do for us?

Ephesians 2:8-9 For by grace you have been saved through faith; and that not of yourselves, it is the gift of God; not as a result of works, that no one should boast.

- In Ephesians 2:8-9, we are saved by grace through what? Can we save ourselves according to this verse? Can we work for salvation?

Walk with God: Discuss... When we talk about being saved, what are we being saved from? Discuss the acrostic for grace – [G – God's; R – Riches; A – At; C – Christ's; E – Expense]. What does it mean to you to receive grace? Remind each other that even our very best day is still dotted with sin and disappointment.

Prayer suggestion... Thank God for grace and salvation. Without the sacrifice of Christ on the cross there is no salvation for man. Thank you, Jesus!

Family Time 2:

Month 11 Topic: God saves us...Are you saved?

Talk with God: Read...Titus 3:5-6

> **Titus 3:5-6 He saved us, not on the basis of deeds which we have done in righteousness, but according to His mercy, by the washing of regeneration and renewing by the Holy Spirit, Whom He poured out upon us richly through Jesus Christ our Savior.**

- Were we saved on the basis of our deeds? Who poured out the Holy Spirit upon us?

Walk with God: Discuss... This Scripture reminds us that our own deeds do not save us. Jesus did it all. Discuss salvation amongst your own family members. Have each of you prayed to receive Jesus Christ into your lives to be saved? Is the Holy Spirit residing in your life (lives)? Here are two questions to consider in discussing salvation: 1) If you were to die tonight, do you know for certain you would spend eternity in Heaven? 2) If you were standing before Jesus and He were to say, "Why should I let you into my Heaven?", what would you say?

Prayer suggestion... Sample prayer of salvation: Lord, I know I am a sinner and I need a Savior. I know you are God and you sent Your Son Jesus to live on this earth, live a perfect life, and die for the sins of the world. I trust You today to save me and come into my heart and live with me for eternity. Thank You, Lord for saving me.

Family Time 3:

Month 11 Topic: God saves us...Saved from what?

Talk with God: Read...Romans 5:9, John 3:16-17

Romans 5:9 We shall be saved from the wrath of God through Him.

- In Romans 5:9, what are we saved from? Through whom?

John 3:16-17 For God so loved the world, that He gave His only begotten Son, that whosoever believes in Him should not perish, but have eternal life. For God did not send the Son into the world to judge the world, but that the world should be saved through Him.

- In John 3:16-17, what did God do as a result of His love for us? If we believe, what will NOT happen?

Walk with God: Discuss... We are saved from the wrath of God. Why did God send Jesus? Discuss the great love a father has for his children. Most parents would give their lives for their children. But would you die for the sins of your neighbors and everyone at your church? Your extended family? People you don't even know? God's love is something we will never know apart from Jesus Christ.

Prayer suggestion... Have each family member thank God for salvation. Pray that your family will know God and His love on a deeper level than ever before.

Family Time 4:

Month 11 Topic: God saves us…Your foundation

Talk with God: Read…Acts 4:10-12, Romans 1:16

> **Acts 4:10-12** Let it be known to all of you, and to all the people of Israel, that by the Name of Jesus Christ the Nazarene, Whom you crucified, Whom God raised from the dead – by this Name this man stands here before you in good health. He is the stone which was rejected by you, the builders, but which became the very Cornerstone. And there is salvation in no one else; for there is no other Name under heaven that has been given among men, by which we must be saved.

- Why, according to Acts 4:10-12, is Jesus called the Cornerstone? Who rejected Him?

> **Romans 1:16** For I am not ashamed of the gospel of Christ, for it is the power of God for salvation to everyone who believes.

- In Romans 1:16, who is offered salvation?

Walk with God: Discuss… In Acts 4:10-12, we know the Cornerstone is Jesus, because the author is telling the listener that *they* rejected the cornerstone. A foundation is built upon a cornerstone. What foundation is your family built upon? Is salvation and your Christian life so important to you that you talk about it to everyone you know? Are you ashamed of the gospel?

Prayer suggestion… Pray that your family will be a light for Christ in your community and not be ashamed.

Family Time 5:

Month 11 Topic: God saves us...Relationship with Jesus

Talk with God: Read...1 Thessalonians 5:9-11

> **1 Thessalonians 5:9-11 For God has not destined us for wrath, but for obtaining salvation through our Lord Jesus Christ Who died for us, that whether we are awake or asleep, we may live together with Him. Therefore encourage one another, and build up one another, just as you also are doing.**

- Did God destine us for wrath? Is eternal life with Christ just for those who have died?

Walk with God: Discuss... God created us for a relationship with Him. He did not create us so that we would perish and be separated forever from Him. That is not God's plan. When we accept Christ into our lives as our Savior, our eternal life with Him begins. How exciting! What does living with Jesus right now look like in your family? How are you growing in your faith and getting to know Him better?

Prayer suggestion... Thank God for eternal life. Thank Him that you are living with Him now and He with you.

Leader Answers:

Family Time 1:

Month 11 Topic: God saves us
Leader Answers:

- Save us
- Faith; no; no
- Discussion ideas: Grace is getting what we don't deserve and not getting what we deserve.

Family Time 2:

Leader Answers:

- No
- Jesus Christ
- Discussion ideas: Use the Romans Road to lead family members through Scripture to explain salvation and believing in Christ: Romans 3:23, Romans 6:23, Romans 5:8, Romans 10:9-11

Family Time 3:

Leader Answers:

- The wrath of God; through Christ
- Gave his only Son; we will not perish (die)
- Discussion ideas: Discuss how hard it would be to give your life for people you didn't know or like. Discuss sacrifice.

Family Time 4:

Leader Answers:

- He is called the Cornerstone because He's the only One Who saves; the people whom He came to save rejected Him
- Everyone who believes

- Discussion ideas: Have family members share how they have been a light in their community, i.e., work, school, neighborhood

Family Time 5:

Leader Answers:

- No; no, for the living, too
- Discussion ideas: Have family members discuss how they feel God working in their lives on a daily basis. What are family members doing to encourage their relationship with Christ? (I.e., devotionals, prayer, service, church attendance, Bible reading, etc.)

MONTH 12

Directions:
As a group, either go through all five "family times" at one time or break it up over four-five weeks, depending on the month.

First – Talk with God

God speaks to you...read the passages and answer the questions.

Reading God's Word, the Holy Bible, is God's way of telling us how to live life. Give Him the time to speak to you. Read the passage first all the way through. Then go back and answer the questions.

Then – Walk with God

Walking... is the action of moving forward with God's instruction from your talk with Him.

And Pray – don't skip this part!

Praying...is your time to talk to God. Prayer is the system that God has designed for you to ask for God's help and you are able to ask because of your relationship with God's only begotten Son, Jesus Christ. If you want to walk with God and hear His direction for you, then you have to ask Him to help you.

For more family activities and devotional ideas to help bring your time in the Word to life, please visit the Sky Ranch Family Devo Resource page. There you will find supplemental activities for each section of the devotional.

www.skyranch.org/familydevoresource

Family Time 1:

Month 12 Topic: God shows us grace...Results of grace

Talk with God: Read...Ephesians 2:7, Ezra 9:8

> **Ephesians 2:7 In order that in the ages to come He might show the surpassing riches of His grace in kindness toward us in Christ Jesus.**

- In Eph 2:7, what does God want to show us?

> **Ezra 9:8 But now for a brief moment grace has been shown from the Lord our God, to leave us an escaped remnant and to give us a peg in His holy place, that our God may enlighten our eyes and grant us a little reviving in our bondage.**

- In Ezra 9:8, what do we receive from God for a brief moment?

- In Ezra 9:8, what does God do as a result of His grace?

Walk with God: Discuss... God's love not only saves us but His love enables Him to show us grace on a daily basis. In the Ezra verse, His grace resulted in enlightenment and revival. What has your family discovered as a result of God's grace?

Prayer suggestion... God, thank You for Your grace on a daily basis. You are kind, Lord, and You have given us a place at Your table. We are thankful.

Family Time 2:

Month 12 Topic: God shows us grace...Walking uprightly

Talk with God: Read...Psalm 84:11-12, Zechariah 12:10

> **Psalm 84:11-12 For the Lord God is a sun and shield; the Lord gives grace and glory; no good thing does He withhold from those who walk uprightly. O Lord of hosts, how blessed is the man who trusts in You!**

- In Psalm 84:11-12, what is God described as? What does He give? From whom does God not withhold one good thing?

> **Zechariah 12:10 And I will pour out on the house of David and on the inhabitants of Jerusalem, the spirit of grace and of supplication, so that they will look on Me Whom they have pierced; and they will mourn for Him, as one mourns for an only son, and they will weep bitterly over Him, like the bitter weeping over a first-born.**

- Zechariah 12:10 says God will pour out what on His people? What will they do as a result of their sin?

Walk with God: Discuss... The Lord is a sun and a shield, as referenced in Psalm 84. What does the sun provide? And a shield? What other inanimate objects could the Lord be described as? Think of as many as you can. Remind each other that God is everything. He provides everything we need. God does not withhold ONE thing from those who love Him and walk uprightly. Why is it hard for family members to walk uprightly some days?

Prayer suggestion... Thank God for His provision and for being your sun and shield.

Family Time 3:

Month 12 Topic: God shows us grace…Encouragement

Talk with God: Read…John 1:17, Acts 11:23, Acts 15:11

> **John 1:17 For the Law was given through Moses; grace and truth were realized through Jesus Christ.**

- In John 1:17, who gave the law? What did Jesus give?

> **Acts 11:23 Then when he had come and witnessed the grace of God, he rejoiced and began to encourage them all with resolute heart to remain true to the Lord.**

- What happened in Acts 11:23, once he had witnessed the grace of God?

> **Acts 15:11 But we believe that we are saved through the grace of the Lord Jesus, in the same way as they also are.**

- Acts 15:11 states that they believe that they are saved through what?

Walk with God: Discuss… The Scriptures remind us that we are saved through grace. We don't deserve salvation. Because of grace we rejoice and encourage and remain true to the Lord. Who have you encouraged today? Who encouraged you?

Prayer suggestion… Thank you, Lord, for sending people to us who encourage us. Thank You for placing people in our path who need encouragement.

Family Time 4:

Month 12 Topic: God shows us grace…Redemption

Talk with God: Read…Romans 3:24, Ephesians 2:5

Romans 3:24 Being justified as a gift by His grace through the redemption which is in Christ Jesus.

- What is the gift we receive in Romans 3:24 because of grace?

- In Rom 3:24, who is redemption in?

Ephesians 2:5 Made us alive together with Christ by grace you have been saved.

- In Eph 2:5, how are we made alive?

Walk with God: Discuss… We are justified, or made right, by grace through redemption in Christ. He redeemed us. He made us right, cleansed us, paid for our sins. Our sins keep us from a relationship with God. Christ redeemed us so that we can have a relationship with God. Grace makes all this possible. What did you do today to make you feel really alive? Give examples.

Prayer suggestion… Thank God you are alive! Every day is a new opportunity to thank Him for all He has done!

Family Time 5:

Month 12 Topic: God shows us grace...Spreading grace

Talk with God: Read...2 Corinthians 4:15, 9:13, 12:9

2 Corinthians 4:15 For all things are for your sakes, that the grace which is spreading to more and more people may cause the giving of thanks to abound to the glory of God.

- In 2 Cor 4:15, why are all things for our sakes?

2 Corinthians 9:13 While they also, by prayer on your behalf, yearn for you because of the surpassing grace of God in you.

- In 2 Cor 9:13, why would people yearn for and pray for you?

2 Corinthians 12:9 And He has said to me, "My grace is sufficient for you, for power is perfected in weakness."

- In 2 Cor 12:9, when is power perfected?

Walk with God: Discuss... Are you spreading God's grace? Have each family member share someone God has laid on their heart that needs to know of the grace of God. What can you do as a family to share God's grace with these people? Invite them to church? Have them over to your home for a meal? Share ideas.

Prayer suggestion... Ask God to use your family to spread the love and grace of God with those you mentioned earlier. Speak each one by name to Him and ask for His help in reaching them for His kingdom.

Leader Answers:

Family Time 1:

Month 12 Topic: God shows us grace
Leader Answers:

- Riches of His grace
- Grace
- Enlightens our eyes and grants us revival in bondage
- Discussion ideas: God's grace is for more than salvation. Grace is merciful kindness, God's favor (blueletterbible.org). Discuss how God is blessing your family in other ways.

Family Time 2:

Leader Answers:

- Sun and shield; grace and glory; those who walk uprightly
- The spirit of grace and supplication; mourn
- Discussion ideas: Discuss peer pressure and cultural pressures.

Family Time 3:

Leader Answers:

- Moses; grace and truth
- Rejoicing and encouragement
- Grace
- Discussion ideas: Why is encouragement so important for the believer? Is it easy being a Christ follower in our culture?

Family Time 4:

Leader Answers:

- Justification
- Christ Jesus

- Through Christ by grace
- Discussion ideas: Talk about redemption. An example could be freedom from guilt of past sins.

Family Time 5:

Leader Answers:

- So that grace will result in thanksgiving and praise
- Because of the grace through Christ they see in you
- In weakness
- Discussion ideas: Make a list of friends you know who don't talk openly about Jesus in their daily life. Sometimes friends don't know Jesus well and don't feel comfortable sharing about Jesus. Others may not know Him personally. Either way, pray for them. Encourage them and invite them into conversations by sharing what Jesus has done for you and the difference He has made in your life and then give them a chance to share too.

OUR LIFE-CHANGING PROGRAMS

Summer Camp: Texas (ages 6-16)

Sky Ranch Summer Camp provides a physical, spiritual and emotional safe haven of amazing fun, incredible adventures and lasting friendships. It's a place where kids will interact with caring counselors who "walk the talk" when it comes to Christian character and moral values. The Summer Camp experience will instill the desire, confidence and wisdom kids need to become everything God created them to be.

COR (1 Corinthians 9:24-27) Leadership Camps - Morph, Quest & Sigma: Texas and Colorado (ages 12-18)

Prayerfully designed to be fresh and relevant, this advanced discipleship program immerses campers in truth and character experiences that help coach teens through the transitions in life. Campers experience new adventures and make new friends while building leadership skills at Sky Ranch's premier camps.

Day Camp: Van, Texas and Dallas, Texas (ages 5-11)

Sky Ranch Day Camp is an awesome daytime camp experience, perfect for kids who aren't quite ready to sleep over for a week but want to get a taste of what camp is like. Kids will love the caring counselors, the five fun-filled days of camp activities and the spiritual investment.

Champions Rodeo Camp & Clinics: Texas

Led by World Champion Steer Wrestler Rope Myers, Sky Ranch Champions Rodeo Camp & Clinics offer general camps for beginning cowboys and cowgirls up to elite clinics for Bull Riding, Steer Wrestling, Team Roping and more. Each rodeo event teaches leadership and discipline to campers in a unique and exciting Christian context.

Wilderness: Colorado

Bring your group to connect with God in the Rocky Mountains of Colorado with Sky Ranch's Wilderness, Backpacking, Kayak Touring or Adventure Trips. Accompanied by our trained guide staff, youth groups will spend four to six nights learning basic mountaineering and low impact camping. This wilderness setting also provides a backdrop for groups to hear one another's story, establish trust, and evaluate their relationship with Christ.

Missions: France and Russia

Sky Ranch's trained ministry team works in partnership with indigenous ministry leaders in France and Russia focusing on evangelism and discipleship through camping experiences.

Family Camp: Colorado (families with kids of all ages)

Located in the beautiful Colorado Rockies, Sky Ranch Ute Trail offers Family Camp to create intentional and purposeful interactions between parent and child. These experiences will refresh the family's spiritual journey and strengthen relationships, all in the beauty and grandeur of the Colorado Rockies. There's something for every member of the family at Sky Ranch Family Camp!

Parent/Child Weekends: Texas

This series of special weekends is designed to create intentional, life-giving connections between parents and their children. Sky Ranch currently offers Father/Son, Mother/Daughter, Father/Daughter and Mother/Son weekend events.

SkyMoms - A Ministry to Moms

SkyMoms provides encouragement, support and education for moms and their families. SkyMoms extends the spirit of Sky Ranch camping discipleship into homes throughout the year to nourish moms so they can better face the daily challenges and opportunities of raising godly kids. In the same way that Sky Ranch invests in the spiritual development of each child, SkyMoms feeds the heart and character of the caretaker! For more information visit www.skyranchskymoms.blogspot.com

Church Camp: Oklahoma

Church Camp at Sky Ranch Cave Springs is like no other! We offer an outstanding experience with first class facilities at an exceptional value for church groups. Whether it is a week day or weekend, two to six night stay you are seeking, we have excellent accommodations for a fantastic get away. Once you've visited Sky Ranch Cave Springs you'll have found a camp home for your group.

Retreats & Conferences: Texas and Oklahoma

Sky Ranch Retreats & Conferences provide the perfect location for any size retreat or conference. Experiences can be tailored to meet the needs of a small group of 15, a family ministry of 150 or a retreat with the capacity up to 900. Sky Ranch's well-trained, servant-minded staff will handle every detail so group leaders and members can focus on enjoying their stay and having a great escape.

School Programs: Texas and On-site

Sky Ranch School Programs provides a variety of educational options for public and private schools including incredible Outdoor Education Programs and on-site school assemblies for leadership training.

For more information,

visit us online at www.SkyRanch.org,
call us at 800.962.2267
or email GuestServices@SkyRanch.org.

facebook.com/SkyRanch

Sky Ranch Friends,

Sky Ranch is committed to the critical task of equipping young people to make life choices that reflect Godly character, passion to impact the kingdom of Christ and desire to prepare the next generation to continue his living legacy. It is our prayer that Sky Ranch never has to turn a child away from the saving knowledge of Jesus Christ.

Sky Ranch is a non-profit ministry that relies on the support of generous donors to provide the necessary funding to support families we serve at our Texas, Oklahoma, and Colorado camps through scholarships. Your donations will help send someone to camp to be part of programs that strengthen kids and their families by sharing the hope of Jesus Christ through the outdoor fun of camping. We hope that you have been blessed by your experience at Sky Ranch and by the Sky Ranch Family Devotionals. If you would like to help us share that experience with others, please donate to our scholarship fund today. You can donate online at www.skyranch.org or cut out the form below and mail it with your gift to Development at Sky Ranch.

You Can Make a Difference in the Life of a Child!

My family would like to give the amount below and help scholarship a camper:

My gift of $_____ ( ) $25 ( ) $50 ( ) $100 ( ) $250 ( ) $500 is enclosed.

( ) I have enclosed my check with a full payment.

( ) I prefer to make my payment by credit card.

( ) Visa   ( ) MasterCard ( ) Discover ( ) American Express

Credit Card #: _____

Exp. Date: _____ CIV Code _____

Name on Credit Card: _____

Signature: _____

First Name: _____ Last Name: _____

Address: _____

City: _____ State: _____ Zip: _____

Phone: _____ Email: _____

Please Mail Your Gift to:
Sky Ranch, Attn: Development Office
500 N. Pearl Street, Suite 640, LB 148
Dallas TX, 75201

Online giving is available at www.SkyRanch.org

Sky Ranch is a 501(c) (3) not-for-profit organization. All gifts are tax-deductible.
We will mail you a receipt for your donation specifying the date and amount.